Crashing the Club:

How I Infiltrated Good Ole Boy Politics, Lost an Election, and Got Famous

---

A Guide to Breaking Barriers, Breaking Rules, and Breaking In

---

By Mande Wilkes

M Media Group

Mande Wilkes

M Media Group

Crashing the Club: How I Infiltrated Good
Ole Boy Politics, Lost an Election, and Got
Famous

A Guide to Breaking Barriers, Breaking Rules, and Breaking In

Copyright ©2011 Mande Wilkes

ISBN-10: 0983739609
ISBN-13: 9780983739609

Printed in the United States of America

<u>ACKNOWLEDGEMENTS</u>

I thank every caustically corrupt South Carolina politician, without whom this book wouldn't have been possible. You know who you are.**

**Names redacted to protect the guilty.

PREAMBLE

So what in the world is a "good ole boy?"

It's been a ubiquitous phrase since the 2010 election cycle, but what does it mean and more importantly, why does it get people so hot and bothered?

Well, a good ole boy isn't really a boy at all, and if he were, he certainly wouldn't be good. (Very often, though, those to whom we refer as good ole boys are indeed old.)

To me, a good ole boy is a symbol—the very essence, in fact—of everything that's wrong with millennial American politics. A good ole boy is like the class tattletale, if the class tattle-tale happened to also be the kid of the teacher of that class. He always appears to be following the rules, and why shouldn't he be? He makes the rules! And most dangerously, he often makes the rules up as he goes, handicapping the rest of us in the game of life.

Usually, the term "good ole boy" is used chiefly in the political context. Politics is certainly a good ole boy's most salient perch, but make no mistake, the good ole boy is everywhere.

Good ole boys are the gatekeepers—of politics, of pop, of any and every nook of life.

Guess what, though?

Society is sick of the gatekeepers and the good ole boys.

More than anything else, the 2012 election cycle will be about identifying and eradicating good ole boys.

But wait, wasn't that the crux of the 2010 election cycle, too?

Let's back up for a moment...

In 2010, people became fed up with the tangled, inaccessible state of American politics, and it dawned on them finally that the good ole boys are to blame.

People wanted their government again to be penetrable, permeable, accessible. From that sprang the Tea Party.

Except...

The good ole boys, patrolling gatekeepers that they are, sensed the cultural zeitgeist regarding accessibility, accountability, and transparency, and they hijacked it. They slapped on it a catchy label that harkened back to America's history—the tea party of the Revolutionary War—and under that brand new brand they sought refuge from the public backlash against the political elite.

And *that's* how the Tea Party was born.

The angry public latched onto the Tea Party movement in hopes of ridding politics of corruption and cronyism. But of course it was a sham, and a shame. Only now is the public beginning to see the Tea Party for what it has become—the bad guys' disguise.

And so 2012 is gearing up to be what 2010 was *supposed* to be—the end of establishment, elitist politics.

As it happened, I came onto the political scene just as the anti-establishment wave was cresting. I thought that meant that I—a neophyte, a newcomer, a novice—had a chance. Obviously, I'd bought into the same narrative into which everybody else had bought.

We weren't all mistaken; we were simply a couple of years ahead of our time. *Now* is the era of blossoming political accessibility; *now* is the era of withering political elitism.

This book is about now and then and then and now—how we got from then to now, and what's next.

INTRODUCTION

The picture message on my phone showed a collection of pill bottles. Sent to me by the wife of a hotshot state official, the accompanying caption scrolled underneath the hazy orange bottles: *He's going to end up dead. Call me please.*

Such was my introduction to the good ole boys club of South Carolina politics.

When I called this wife of a "good ole boy," she was nice to me—certainly nicer than she'd been the day she intercepted a cryptic voicemail I'd left at her husband's office; or the day she crashed a debate between my opponent and me and lobbed me barbed questions; or the day she showed up at my husband's store seeking solidarity, circling and highlighting entries in her own husband's phone records and advising that she and my husband ally.

And she was certainly nicer to me than the good ole boys themselves. For their part, they fit into one of two camps: (1) Indignant or (2) begrudgingly welcoming.

The indignant ones disliked that I was crashing their club. Here I was, 25 years old, unknown and unproven. Of all the things I was not, the most threatening was that I was *uncorrupted*. I had no allegiances. I had no legacy, other than the one that I was right then concocting. That terrified them, and why shouldn't it? If I was uncorrupted, how could they know what to leverage? Without knowing which of my strings were which, they couldn't engage in their usual puppetry.

Such was the conundrum of the indignant good ole boys.

But what about the welcoming ones? Well, as I said, *begrudgingly* welcoming.

For their part, they weren't indignant because they were at least peripherally aware of the bigger picture. Recalling Sarah Palin and Hilary Clinton, they looked at me and they sensed a zeitgeist, and they thought that if they played their cards right they could ride the wave.

Resistant as they were to change, they didn't blind themselves to it. Like the indignant ones, they resented that I hadn't "paid my dues." But they feigned support, offering me fundraising lists (*outdated* fundraising lists, a fact I discovered when virtually all of my outgoing electoral mail came back undelivered) and introducing me to influential strategists and advisors (all of whom I later confirmed as being moles for my opponent).

By the way, speaking of political strategists and advisers, most of them got into that business after losing their own campaign(s). I too lost, but I parlayed my loss into a book deal and a television show, not an advising gig. I don't understand political strategy, and I don't pretend to. Put down this book right now (in fact, return it for a refund) if what you're looking for is sound campaign strategy. Remember, people, I lost my campaign!

Herein you won't learn how to win an election. In fact, I won't guarantee that you'll learn anything at all. (Hey, maybe you spent your formative years in South Carolina public schools – not my fault!) If not necessarily educational, this guide is certainly entertaining, shocking, and provocative, because even the vicarious act of crashing a club entertains, shocks, and provokes.

If you do learn something (and I hope you do, otherwise you might not buy my next book, forcing me to get a *real* job), what you'll learn is how to *crash the club*. You'll learn how to crash **any** club. Be it politics, business, publishing, a particular social circle, a snooty HOA board, or any other "exclusive" menagerie of movers and shakers, herein you just might learn how to pierce the veil of insularity.

Mande Wilkes

BE ETHNIC.

(PREFERABLY HISPANIC.)

🙂

"After *Zorro*, people spoke Spanish to me for ages. I'm Welsh but that movie instantly gave me a new ethnicity."

--Catherine Zeta Jones

THE LOWDOWN

Quick! Take a look at my photo on the book jacket. Do you wonder "what" I am? Hispanic, maybe? I'm not—I'm an Israeli Jew with Eastern European roots, for what it's worth—but South Carolina Republicans don't differentiate among ethnicities. 'Round these parts, ethnic is ethnic.

Seizing on the Republican Party's blossoming "big tent" theme, my evident ethnic-ness was heralded as "just what the Party needs."

A Republican Party county chairman was enthused that I, "a Latina," was campaigning for elected office. "A Latina," he hoped, would spur the "big tent" movement in South Carolina, demonstrating that there are some Republicans who are not, in fact, Caucasian, geriatric, and male.

The chairman was hardly the only one with such delusions of my grandeur.

At a pre-election potluck forum, the organizer tactfully (tackily?) let me know that I was welcome to bring guacamole if I didn't know how to cook chicken bog. Cross my heart and hope to die, she actually said that.

And at a gubernatorial candidate's Christmas party, the candidate himself invited me to join in the caroling with a solo performance of "Feliz Navidad." Fortunately, "dreidel, dreidel, dreidel" turned out to be ethnic enough. (Actually, I'm pretty sure this earned me bonus points: "Look, y'all!..a Mexican Jew!")

THE LESSON

Minority rules.

Sometimes I call it the Oppression Olympics©. Sometimes I call it the Race for Disenfranchised Firsts©. Whatever you want to call it, the bottom line is that, in millennial America, minorities rule. Ethnicity is the simplest way to distinguish yourself as a minority. But even if your appearance isn't at least potentially ethnic, pretty much everybody can identify themselves as a minority of some sort. Seriously. I don't care if you're blue-eyed, blonde-haired, and fair-skinned—if that's the case, call yourself a refugee…of the sun. Hell, if all else fails, say that you're autistic and call it a day.

Being "ethnic" endears you to the powers-that-be while simultaneously disarming those very people in power. In other words, the "good ole boys" will welcome you because that's the politically correct thing to do, but they won't think you matter enough to threaten their established status quo.

Endear. Disarm. Infiltrate. Seize.

BE A LADY...

(AND A TRAMP.)

I'm always rather nervous about how you talk about women who are active in politics, whether they want to be talked about as women or as politicians.

--John F. Kennedy

THE LOWDOWN

Being female is especially handy when trying to crash the club. That's because, in politics as in pop, all eyes are on the girl in the group.

Is that politically incorrect? Oops.

Fact is, any candidate for any office is likely male. I mean that not as an indictment against either men or politics, but as a statement of absolute truth. In fact, excepting Girl Scouts of America and maybe Kotex Inc., pretty much all organizations are populated by men.

And that's *awesome* for women.

Why? Because a woman among men is a candidate automatically distinguished. All eyes are on her, automatically. And where our eyes go, our votes (or dollars, or support) follow.

So to kick off my campaign, I blanketed my district with 8' x 12' billboards of my photo. Where eyes go, votes follow, remember? At every traffic intersection, at every crosswalk, at every neighborhood entrance, all eyes were on me.

When I launched my campaign TV commercials, my ad was one among dozens of campaign spots—but I was the sole female. We notice that which stands out ... and stand out I did, among the cadre of good ole boys in their television ads. Our respective financial disclosure reports indicate that my opponent and I spent equivalent money on TV commercials, but by sheer saliency, I got a hell of a lot more bang for my buck.

THE LESSON

It's not enough to simply be female. Half the planet is female, after all. It's certainly helpful to be a lady, but you've also got to be a tramp …so to speak.

To be a tramp is to leverage gender, make it an asset, use it as collateral, invest its dividends.

Being the right kind of tramp is mostly about emphasis and exaggeration. You want to constantly do things to remind people that you're a girl. Wear your gender as your insignia: Let that be the basis of your brand.

When I shot my commercial, I had my makeup professionally applied. It turned out that my professionally applied makeup made me resemble a corpse. On camera especially, I looked *bad*. I knew I looked like a nightmare, so I reshot the commercial…but I chose to run the "ugly" one for two days, even though I looked astronomically better in the second spot. By running first the ugly and then the pretty commercials, I created a "before-and-after" moment, thereby reminding people I was a girl by making them fo-

cus on my horrid makeup. It worked! Dozens—
literally, dozens—of women told me at the precincts on the day of the election that they'd no-
ticed the difference between the ads.

A woman, almost by definition, is not one of the
good ole boys, and that's precisely her "in." The
lady who is a tramp *will* crash the club.

Mande Wilkes

BE BUSY.

A bee is never as busy as it seems; it's just that it can't buzz any slower.

--Kin Hubbard

THE LOWDOWN

Just several weeks before the election, I was a no-show to the single largest electoral event in the county. Along with my own opponent, every last one of the other candidates were in attendance. Local and statewide candidates alike were there.

Though I'd confirmed my attendance weeks before, I issued a last-minute statement of apology:

"Regrettably, I cannot attend this evening's event. I'm currently otherwise engaged with commitments to the constituency, and cannot break away. I'm confident the event will be a success, and that it will excite and engage Republican voters ahead of next month's election."

In other words, my memo declared that I was too damn busy to mingle with the riffraff. In reality, I spent the evening in my hammock, reading an Ayn Rand biography. I was certainly occupied, but I was hardly busy. But the perception was that I was busy—too busy to attend a possibly make-or-break event—and that perception fed the perception that I was far more legitimate than I actually was.

That was my most egregious act of truancy, but it certainly wasn't my only. Throughout the campaign season I regularly skipped out on all kinds of events, always with the excuse that I just couldn't manage to break away from my responsibilities. Naturally, this made my life sound exceedingly interesting and full, and so it made me sound remarkable and important. It made me sound, in a word, *unbeatable.*

THE LESSON

☞

Don't go to every single party, fundraiser, happy hour, get-together, meeting, quorum, debate, or forum. In fact, skip most networking events. More important than playing hooky, however, is to tell a key person that you can't attend.

Oh, and while you're talking to that key person, abruptly end the phone call. *"I'm so sorry, I have to take this other line. International call, don't want to miss it. Hate that I can't be there tonight, give my regards to John. Bye!"*

And while you're at it, now and again it's useful to activate the "away" setting in your email account. This function will automatically send "I'm away" emails in response to emails sent to you. Personalize it if you like—"I'm in Tahiti" or "I'm on spiritual sabbatical" or "I'm recuperating from a facelift—or simply say "I'm away." It's not important what you're doing; what's important is that you are important enough to put everybody on hold at your whim.

Sure, this type of behavior comes off as contemptible, entitled, and arrogant. Busy people get flack, but they also get deference.

Mande Wilkes

BE SHAMELESS.

"A man has to be Joe McCarthy to be ruthless. All a woman has to do is put you on hold."

--Marlo Thomas

THE LOWDOWN

"Here's a hundred dollars for your re-election campaign. By the way, I'll be running against you."

That's right…my opponent was the first to whom I announced my candidacy. I handed him that news, and then I handed him a check for his campaign.

Everybody who wanted me to win—consultants, supporters, my own family—thought I'd lost my mind. They were frantic with worry that voters would get wind of my contribution-*cum*-campaign. They asked me how I was ever going to defend the fact that I'd contributed money to my opponent's campaign and then launched a bid against him.

Then began the buzz about my speech at a Tea Party gala, and everybody stopped worrying. (Well, everybody in my camp stopped worrying. Everybody in *his* camp started worrying in earnest.)

"Good evening ladies and gentleman. I'm Man-de Wilkes, and I want to let you in on a secret. A few weeks ago I contributed money to my opponent's re-election campaign...and then I checked into his voting record. I couldn't believe what I saw! Here was a man—a very nice man, for what it's worth—who runs as a Republican but leads like a liberal. That's why I decided to enter the race. I couldn't stand the thought of the voters continuing to be misled, misrepresented, and miserable. So that's my dirty little secret: I contributed money to my opponent's campaign, and it was the best $100 I ever wasted."

The Tea Parties ate it up! It was as populist a sentiment as ever there was: I'd been deceived by a politician, and I was fighting back.

THE LESSON

In reality, though, I was the deceptive one. Well, I wasn't actually deceptive—I didn't lie or misrepresent. No, I didn't deceive anyone. I was crafty...shamelessly crafty. I'd counted on my clueless opponent to cash my check, and when he did I got every penny's worth of the benefit of my bargain.

Here's the thing: Even though it sounds rather Machiavellian, all I really did was a little bit of maneuvering.

Crashing the club is all about exploiting delusions of invincibility.

Had my opponent foreseen my shenanigans, he could have nipped me in the bud by simply not cashing my check. But it didn't occur to him that I had something up my sleeve. He chalked my check up to what he perceived as weirdness, blowing me off because he didn't see me—an outsider, a newcomer—as a threat.

The various gatekeepers—the incumbents, the chairmen of the board, the directors and the "deciderers" and the doyens—are sure that they're invincible by virtue of their status. To crash the club, it's your job to shamelessly exploit those delusions of invincibility.

Mande Wilkes

PROCRASTINATE.

"If you're playing a poker game and you look around the table and can't tell who the sucker is, it's you."

--Paul Newman

THE LOWDOWN

True story: I waited until just three weeks before the election to start campaigning.

To put that in perspective, candidates typically campaign for *months* before the election. And remember that I was up against a three-term incumbent…by industry standards that alone necessitated an early start.

I got such a late start, in fact, that the good ole boys were confident that I'd chickened out. But while I was looking like a chicken, I was thinking like a fox.

After a long period of apparent inactivity on my part, my team went in the middle of the night one Friday night and absolutely blanketed the district with Wilkes for House paraphernalia. That Saturday morning, with my signs and banners and pamphlets everywhere, there was no longer any doubt that I was running. Billboards of my face easily dwarfed my opponent's signs.

Seriously, it was like how on Thanksgiving Day there's no evidence of Christmas, and then the day after Thanksgiving, it's Christmas everywhere you look.

That's how I did it: As far as anyone could tell, I had no campaign…and then, like a political piñata, I exploded all over my district.

THE LESSON

An early start is always the industry standard. But the industry standard, by definition, is designed to maintain the status quo.

Club-crashers lack the luxury of an early start, because club-crashers simply can't afford a protracted battle with the good ole boys.

Had I heeded conventional wisdom and been the "early bird" in the race, I would have been forced to go tit-for-tat with the establishment machine…and there's no possible way to match the establishment's money and resources.

By procrastinating, I avoided an expensive tit-for-tat battle and, just as importantly, I put my opponent on the defensive. He was too busy defending against my sudden onslaught to mount a campaign of his own. By that point, every move he made came across as a jumbled response to me.

BE VAIN.

"Don't be humble ... you're not that great."

--Golda Meir

THE LOWDOWN

A few hours after the voting precincts closed, while watching election returns with my family, a newspaper reporter called me for a statement. At that point, even though vote counts were still straggling in, it was pretty clear that my opponent had just barely won.

Naturally, I was expected to issue a statement in which I acknowledged my loss and humbly congratulated my opponent. They in the biz call it a "concession statement."

I didn't exactly concede, though. What I did was I declared to the reporter my candidacy for the following election cycle—which was then more than two years away.

I hadn't even officially lost the race, and there I was hurling my hat in the ring again.

And as if that weren't egregious enough, the candidacy I declared was for U.S. Congress. That's right…I'd just gone from losing a state House race to running for U.S. Congress.

Who did I think I was??

THE LESSON

I'm not an ambitious person. In fact, ambition bores me.

Vanity is often mistaken for ambition, but really, they're opposite characteristics.

Ambition is a value; vanity is a state of mind. In other words, ambition is instilled while vanity is cultivated. In *other* other words, ambitious people care about meeting goals and vain people care about announcing goals.

Vanity is essential for the club-crasher. Infiltrating the establishment requires you to abandon ambition, because—believe it or not—ambition will hold you back.

Ambitious people care about achieving goals. Vain people care about announcing goals. See, it's not about being a Congresswoman. Ambitious people need to be in Congress. Ambitious people won't stop until they accomplish what they set out to do, whether it be in politics or otherwise. Ambitious people achieve by winning, while vain people achieve no matter what, win or lose.

Because of my post-election newspaper announcement, the good ole boys accuse me of blind ambition. But if I were ambitious, I'd have been concerned with saving face in the wake of defeat. Ambition leads you to avoid loss; vanity encourages you to leverage loss.

KNOW YOUR AUDIENCE.

☺ ☺ ☹

"We are not trying to entertain the critics. I'll take my chances with the public."

--Walt Disney

THE LOWDOWN

Once upon a time I was a contributing editor with South Carolina's premier political online media outlet. Actually, my official position at the company was "Agent Provocateur." Officially, that was my title.

True to the title of the position, I had fun with it, occasionally approaching my pieces from the perspective of a gonzo journalist. That meant a lot of gratuitous pictures of me, and that also meant some controversial articles in which I posited, for example, that breast cancer is a feminist farce, or that the movie *Dirty Dancing* is, according to today's quirky standards, a tale of pedophilia.

I was publishing these articles around the same time that I was considering a run for public office. Of course, everybody who was anybody wagged their finger at me, warning me that my youthful recklessness would be forever archived on the annals of the Web. Seriously, the political establishment was positively apocalyptic in its certainty that my journalistic musings would make my political career dead on arrival.

But I kept writing.

When the time came for me to define myself to voters, I termed myself a contributing editor and political reporter.

THE LESSON

Guess what? The voters didn't terribly mind my provocative online presence. On the contrary, it humanized me. Some people were offended by my opinions, sure, but they didn't hold it against me at the polls.

Knowing your audience means knowing who you can afford to offend. Once you've figured out whose sensibilities you can assault, your parameters are drawn.

Most of the time, it's the good ole boys who are endlessly offended. Everybody else just wants to be entertained. So entertain the people who matter to your mission, and to hell with anybody else.

It's a matter of keeping your eye on the ball. To entertain and engage your audience, you have to know who your audience is…and who your audience isn't.

FLAUNT YOUR WEALTH

(OR FAKE IT.)

$$$

"In the beginning there was nothing. God said, "let there be light!" And there was light. There was still nothing, but you could see it a whole lot better."

--Ellen DeGeneres

THE LOWDOWN

Money talks, so every time I'd talk about running for office, the good ole boy network would try to stifle me with warnings of the steep cost of a campaign. Money talks, so I'd respond with a shrug of my shoulders and a "so what"?

To add insult to their injury, I made sure to avoid the conventional fundraising circles, and I slammed candidates who took out bank loans to finance their campaigns.

The establishment was stunned: Here I was, a 25-year old candidate who ostensibly cared not a bit how much it cost me to run. And, even more peculiarly, I didn't even appear to be seeking financial backers.

In reality, I *was* fundraising—but my contributors weren't part of the political machine, so nobody knew the tens of thousands of dollars I was raking in. (In fact, as of this writing, I make sure to maintain a balance of more than $10,000 in my campaign account…just so I can every now and then mention it to the good ole boys who are diligently trying to dissuade me from a Congressional run.)

THE LESSON

☞

Here's the thing about money: For purposes of crashing the club, the important thing is that there's an *illusion* of wealth.

It's entirely irrelevant whether or not you've got money to burn. Create the *illusion* that you're able and willing to outspend anybody else, and just like that, you've bought yourself a reputation. Just like that, you've simultaneously intimidated challengers and branded yourself a juggernaut.

It really is that simple, with one caveat:

When it comes time to spend money on your cause, feign extreme reluctance to part with your wealth.

That—deliberative parsimony—will cement the illusion of wealth.

Because the thing about rich people is that they're cheap as hell. So if all you're doing is running around acting carefree about money, you risk looking like a fake and a flake. To cinch the illusion, you have to pretend you're scared to spend. What I did was I met with virtually every political consultant in the state, and within fifteen minutes of each meeting I told each of them I wouldn't accept their fee structure.

Money talks. Frugality screams.

Mande Wilkes

REFUSE TO

FOLLOW

THROUGH.

❌

"Politics is the gentle art of getting votes from the poor and campaign funds from the rich by promising to protect each from the other."

--Oscar Ameringer

Mande Wilkes

THE LOWDOWN

I graduated law school several years ago, but I've yet to become licensed to practice law.

When defining myself to voters, I deemed myself a "legal consultant." Get it? Because you don't need a license to consult. And because "legal consultant" sounds really good to people who are sick and tired of voting for lawyers, don't you think?

THE LESSON

Framing is everything.

More than simply turning lemons into lemonade, framing is an art. It's about sensing public sentiment and seizing on it.

Even if I had a license to practice law, I still would have called myself a legal consultant rather than a lawyer. More than merely a lawyer, legal consultants are dynamic and also full of mystique (what does a consultant actually *do*, anyway?).

By figuring out how to frame my lack of licensing, I bypassed voter cynicism and defined myself in accordance with the times.

Mande Wilkes

BECOME ONE OF
THEM.

"If voting changed anything, they'd make it illegal."

--Emma Goldman

THE LOWDOWN

The day after the election—literally hours after I'd lost the race—the driver of the car next to me honked at me. (My car was still plastered with my campaign stickers; it wasn't hard to pick me out of a crowd at a red light.) He said he had voted for me because he'd hoped to be part of a revolution to get rid of the good ole boys.

It dawned on me, right there at that red light, that it takes an establishment to rival an establishment.

So I yelled at him from my car window: "I'm forming a group of like-minded reformers…want to join?"

As soon as I got home, I blasted an email to my most rabid supporters, enlisting them to be a part of that emerging establishment.

THE LESSON

Crashing the club is at its core about offering an alternative.

If American enterprise is rooted in the phrase "build it and they will come," then American politics is rooted in the phrase "the more, the merrier." More than anything, people want to be *part* of something. By forming a political action group, I've invited people to contribute themselves to the cause.

And that's exactly how establishments are built—gradually, eventually, inevitably. Today's political grassroots start-up is tomorrow's political juggernaut.

Too often, reformers are insular and exclusive. Ironically, insularity and exclusivity are exactly what's wrong with the good ole boy system, but somehow a lot of reformers fail to connect those particular dots.

You can't reverse the entire corrupt system on your own. You get rid of the establishment by becoming one, and the only way to do that is to recruit, embrace, and invite like-minded people.

BE PART OF A
SEX SCANDAL.

☞

"An affair wants to spill, to share its glory with the world. No act is so private it does not seek applause."

--John Updike

THE LOWDOWN

As I've already mentioned herein, leading up to my race I was a contributing editor with a premiere political website founded and run by the then-governor's former spokesman, Will Folks. A few weeks before the election, news broke of an alleged erstwhile affair between Folks and gubernatorial candidate Nikki Haley. (Now *Governor* Nikki Haley, as it were.)

Folks was slandered and slammed for coming out with news of the affair just weeks before Haley's election date. Besides Folks, I was the face of the website…and so I could have easily been minced into collateral damage, poisoned by my proximity to the scandal.

So what I did was I feigned over-the-top paranoia about that very risk.

When talking on the phone to anyone remotely connected to politics, I spoke obliquely, warning in hushed tones that because of my involvement, my phone was likely being tapped by the major news wires and maybe even state law enforcement officials.

I posted cryptic messages on Facebook, messages that gave the illusion that I was worried that I myself could become embrangled in the scandal. One such message alluded ever so vaguely to a photo depicting me in a ménage-a-trois.

I even carried on these shenanigans with my own campaign adviser, just to keep him invested and intrigued and on his toes.

Of course, my phone was not being tapped. And of course there was no such incriminating picture. In fact, at the time of the alleged Folks-Haley affair, I'd never even heard of their names nor had they heard of mine.

THE LESSON

Though I couldn't have been less involved with the alleged Folks-Haley affair, my strategic insinuations of involvement lent gravitas to my campaign. By placing myself within proximity of the whole mess, I reaped the benefits without suffering the sting of a scandal.

Especially among the good ole boys, this was a successful strategy on my part. If I myself had been involved in the scandal, and if I was indeed at risk of being exposed, who would I bring down with me?

Club-crashing is, if nothing else, the art of finding the intersection between self-preservation and self-promotion.

A sex scandal—yours or otherwise—strikes that balance, simultaneously shrouding and spotlighting you.

BE A COPYCAT.

©

"Men often applaud an imitation and hiss the real thing."

--Aesop

THE LOWDOWN

Though I don't need eyeglasses, the first move I made as a candidate was to buy a pair of snazzy non-prescription frames. I wore them anytime I addressed a group, and I wore them in the photos in my campaign literature.

Why?

Because the takeaway message of Sarah Palin's meteoric rise was that maybe men don't make passes at girls who wear glasses, but they sure do vote for them.

Sure enough, the eyeglasses resonated. All the time, people compared me to Palin. Simply by accessorizing like a political superstar, I'd validated my place in politics. (The reason I know that copycatting worked for me was because my detractors, to their credit, called me on it … which meant that they themselves associated with the decade's biggest political celebrity.)

THE LESSON

From childhood we're taught that originality is paramount, and that copycatting is a sign that we have nothing to offer. But to get to a place of originality, first we have to be willing to be derivative.

Indeed, there's nothing truly unique. Even—especially!—the most seemingly singular idea was hatched elsewhere.

For a club-crasher, copycatting is absolutely crucial: You take from the establishment cues about what works, what sells, what resonates...and then you figure out how to flip that formula in your favor.

And make no mistake, every industry—politics, pop, and beyond—has a formula. The formula works. Trust the formula. Trust the formula, and then tweak the formula. **Tweaking the formula is where you make the leap from derivative to original.**

Mande Wilkes

BE
INACCESSIBLE.

"A celebrity is a person who works hard all of their life to become well-known, and then wears dark glasses to avoid being recognized."

--Fred Allen

Mande Wilkes

THE LOWDOWN

Contrary to every piece of political counsel I received, I didn't create a Facebook account until just a few weeks before the date of the election.

Actually, that's not entirely true. I'd had a Facebook account for years—since law school—but I deleted it a few months before the election. Not because I wanted to shield myself from social media faux pas. Hardly!

I deleted the account—and then waited until practically the last minute to revive it—in order to create the illusion of inaccessibility.

THE LESSON

In the age of insta-comm, wearing out your welcome is an inevitability.

Interest is a function of mystique. I think that's why AMC's television hit *Mad Men* is so universally appealing: In the 1960's, people were permitted their curiosities.

And when it comes down to it, curiosity is the currency of compensation.

People want to wonder. So, for Heaven's sake, let them wonder!

Let your voicemail fill up so that callers can't leave a message. Maintain a Twitter account but seldom tweet. Let Facebook friend requests dangle for weeks. Declare email bankruptcy by sending a mass mailing notifying all your contacts that, due to your inbox volume, you're hereby deleting all unopened mail and starting from scratch.

The good ole boys are constantly in your face. Indeed, that's the very factor that makes them the good ole boys. They're always accessible.

They're always *there*. The club-crasher is just the opposite: *Not* there.

BEFRIEND A
KEY MEMBER
OF THE
ESTABLISHMENT.

"Charm is the way of getting the answer 'yes' without asking a clear question."

--Albert Camus

THE LOWDOWN

As much as I slam the establishment, the truth is that I have lasting and enriching friendships with two bona fide good ole boys.

Though these are now personally important friendships, I have to admit that they began as a ~~calculated~~ strategic move on my part.

THE LESSON

You can't possibly crash the club unless you understand the culture of the club. That seems logical enough, right?

You need somebody to show you the ropes and to explain the intra-establishment pecking order. And, of course, you need somebody to make introductions.

I can't emphasize enough how vital it is to be introduced to the establishment by a fellow member of the establishment. It's this that sets you apart from the fanatics and the amateur renegades.

Alone, I would have appeared to be a fringe interloper. Instead, bookended as I was by my two establishment friends, I represented revolution and reform with gravitas and legitimacy. Appearing to belong—looking like you fit right in—is essential. The world is full of wrongheaded rebels who don't recognize that to win the game, you've got to play the game.

BE A

VICTIM.

**"There is no female Mozart because
there is no female Jack the Ripper."**

--Camille Paglia

THE LOWDOWN

Days before my opponent and I were due to debate, he sent out a district-wide mailing that deemed me a "Jill-in-the-box." (Get it? "Jill"…because I'm a girl. Geez.)

I'm pretty sure the clever turn of phrase was lost on the electorate, but as I understood it, his point was that whoever voted for me couldn't be sure what they'd end up getting.

His message was basically that I wasn't a good ole boy—indeed, I wasn't a boy at all!—and so I couldn't be trusted.

THE LESSON

There's nothing "the people" hate more than being reminded that they're mere cogs in the mega-machine of life. That's where my opponent went wrong with his "Jill-in-the-box" memo. In calling me out for being a newcomer, he was also calling out every voter. After all, if his message was correct, I was exactly like the voters themselves: An outsider who simply wanted a voice.

And so, on the day of the debate, I sent a campaign staffer to a toy store and asked him to buy a Jack-in-the-box. (He didn't blink an eye, God bless him, though I'm pretty sure that was beyond the scope of his job description.)

Anyway, I showed up at the debate with my Jack-in-the-box and I wound it up for the audience until out popped Jack, and then I took out a tube of lipstick and I painted Jack's mouth red and I held it up to the crowd. I told the audience that this was how my opponent saw anyone— especially a *girl*—who dared to offer voters an alternative to the failed status quo.

I played the part of the victim—a victim of my opponent's flagrant sexism and elitism, and a victim of the sexist and elitist system as a whole. Sure I was pandering (generally, I'm hardly one to whine about discrimination) but sometimes you have to play dead now to play at all later.

BE A CLICHÉ.

"Originality is the fine art of remembering what you heard but forgetting where you heard it."

--Laurence J. Peter

THE LOWDOWN

Even as I struck blow after blow against the established process, I capitalized on every imaginable cliché. I appropriated phrases like "failed status quo" and "same-old, same-old" and—lo and behold—"good ole boy".

Even my central campaign promises were trite talking points: Term limits; school choice; tax reduction; spending caps.

THE LESSON

For now and forevermore, *reform* (or "change," as President Barack Obama so poignantly put it) is the point of politics.

Reform is a club-crasher's ticket in! Too often, though, the real reformers—the club-crashers themselves—are so hell-bent on changing the rules that they ignore the power of time-tested formulas.

In politics as in pop, daring to be different is all well and fine, as long as you're not so different that you veer from what people know and trust.

Speaking of pop, Lady Gaga is a reformer if ever there was one. But as different as she dares to be, there's one thing she does exactly like every other singer in the world: She sings about love, because she realizes that she can't reverse the winning boy-meets-girl cliché. So she leverages the cliché by building her brand around what works. She can afford to be different, in other words, because in one key area she's exactly the same.

Being a reformer doesn't mean starting from scratch, because starting from scratch means snatching from people what they know and trust. Use the clichés to create the context within which you can be different. Permit people their clichés.

AFTERWORD

∞

There's something in the air.

Americans have awoken to the corruption that permeates every level of politics and poisons our very way of life.

That's why I wrote this book. Encouraged by the dawning determination to preserve Americana, I wanted to share what it's like to go head-to-head with the corrupt political establishment.

Too often, this is a topic that devolves into cynicism and gloom. Understandably, people feel that the corruption is so entrenched that there's no use in fighting back.

But what I hope you take from this book is that the status quo is not eternal—or at least it doesn't have to be. What I hope you take from this book is that you can carve out a nook for yourself even in the most unwelcoming of places.

Indeed, the concept of "crashing the club" goes beyond the political realm. Crashing the club is more than a concept, in fact…it's an *ideal*, and it's the bedrock of Americana.

Anytime there is social upheaval in Europe or the Mideast or elsewhere, I watch on the news as ordinary people protest corruption and demand democracy. From the relative comfort of our couches, it's easy to look down on that kind of chaos, complacent in the knowledge that "those things" don't happen in America.

But to discount the value of dissent is to concede our very culture.

Don't get me wrong…I'm not bashing our country. If anything, in fact, what I'm suggesting is that the American experiment has worked so well that we've forgotten how to respond to a government that is broken. What I'm suggesting is that, for most of this nation's history, our government has been *ours*…and so we are out of practice when it comes to curing the political ills that are right now infecting our government.

What this means is that while we have a lot more than those third-world political dissenters, we also have a lot more to lose. And so even though we feel the unraveling of American ideals, we're still in the process of figuring out how to fix a government that is failing us.

The reason Americans don't take to the streets in revolt is because we worry about cutting off our noses to spite our faces, so to speak. Despite all that is going wrong in our government, life in the U.S. remains just comfortable enough—and

Mande Wilkes

certainly more comfortable than it'd be if we were to demand a revolution.

But that's just it...*revolt* is the base word of *revolution.*

What we have to do, then, is to redefine revolt. That's why I wrote this book. Preserving the American way of life is about much more than reforming government. It's about reshaping society.

Government is such an insidious aspect of any society that a corrupt government can mean nothing but a corrupt culture. Every institution of American culture—politics, pop, academia, media, clergy, business, medicine—has been corrupted, its leaders inculcated with an air of entitlement and aristocracy. This aversion to outsiders has created what feels like an unbreakable bubble into which we can't even see.

That's exactly how it felt when I decided to run for public office. I felt handicapped: Deafened by the establishment and paralyzed by the process. Of course I lost the election!

Now probably seems like a good time for a turning point of sorts: The point at which I allude to lessons learned and happy endings, the point where I say something about having lost but not feeling lost anymore.

You know what, though? At the time of this writing, I'm considering a Congressional campaign...and I feel like just as much of an underdog as before. Already the establishment is trying to trample me. Just this morning, in fact, I got an email from an entrenched state senator, the subject of which was what he called my "sustained ignorance of federal policy."

Well, the cornerstone of federal policy remains the Declaration of Independence and I'm pretty familiar with *that* . . .

In fact, that's kind of what this book is...a declaration of independence from the establishment itself. And I'm hardly alone.

The sentiment—rejection of the failed status quo and willful defiance of those who perpetuate it—is all the rage right now, creating reformers out of everyday people.

Consider Michele Bachmann, the sharp-tongued congresswoman from Minnesota who is, at the time of this writing, poised for the presidency.

Bachmann's meteoric rise has been anything but traditional. She's been, since pretty much the day she took her oath, *persona non grata* among the Washington, D.C. elite. Why? Well, because her congressional career has been punctuated by a series of "gaffes". That's how the establishment refers to her pointed remarks, at least. The rest of us simply consider her a tell-it-like-it-is American who just so happens to be a member of Congress.

And that—her capacity to offend—is why she is right now resonating with Americans who want desperately to elect outsiders but who are rarely, if ever, given the choice.

Sarah Palin struck a chord with the country for the same reason—her ability to call the good ole boys on their B.S.

Speaking of Palin…where is she, anyway? How come I'm seemingly discussing her as an afterthought? Shouldn't she be the very poster woman of renegade politics?

Well, Palin did such a good job of beating the establishment at its own game—she so handily rooted her way into the institution—that there's the perception among many that she herself is as much a part of the problem as the actual good ole boys. In other words, a lot of people are having a hard time believing that Palin is the political outsider that she once was. In other *other* words, Palin has lost some of her momentum because Americans seem to understand intuitively that there's truth to that thing about lying with dogs and getting fleas.

And that right there is the big catch-22 of crashing the club. Once you're in, then what?

That's really what this book is about, at its core.

Michele Bachmann has out-Palin'd Palin—has in fact eclipsed her in terms of presidential potential—because while Palin continues to beef up her political *bona fides*, Bachmann remains raw. Since losing the 2008 vice presidency, Palin has worked hard to shed her airhead image. Her creation of a Political Action Committee in particular was a strategic move on her part to appear more politically viable. Palin's PAC, together with her alliance with FOX News, phenomenal fundraising capacity, and her bestselling memoirs, have branded her as a politician. Which would be a good thing for her career, except that the basis of her appeal was that she was the un-candidate. Bachmann, in contrast, has only played up the "flake factor" since announcing her candidacy for president.

So Sarah Palin would indeed have been the poster woman of a club-crashing politician, if only she hadn't gone and made herself resemble a member of the elite. But Bachmann's approach risks going too far in the opposite direction.

That's why the whole thing is such a delicate balancing act: The art of aggravating without alienating. Of course, the inclination for most wannabe politicians is to not aggravate at all, but frankly if that's your inclination then you bought the wrong book and I'm surprised you're still reading.

I've dedicated a good chunk of this book to the art of aggravating, so here I'll spend some time on the topic of aggravating without alienating. Because if all you want to do is piss off the good ole boys, you too are reading the wrong book.

The establishment is the establishment because it has put into place a complex system to guarantee that the status quo remains just that. What that means is that it's up to the club-crasher, once "in," to figure out how to finagle the system without alienating the elite. In practical terms, what I'm saying is that the establishment won't be dissolved so much as managed.

For example, for all my chatter about preserving Americana, I have to admit that my House race didn't actually rid South Carolina of its establishment woes. Not even close! What it did, though, was it laid the foundation for the platform on which I stand now, the platform on which I invite you to stand too.

That's what the concept of crashing the club is all about—lasting adjustments to the system, a bottom-up approach to rooting out corruption, elitism, and nepotism.

Establishment politics corrodes our culture by refusing access to outsiders. Such systematic insularity excludes the very people it purports to serve. Here the evergreen political phrase "out of touch" comes to mind: The very elected officials whose jobs is it to represent us speak not on behalf of us but on behalf of their own corrupted interests.

The people we elect are supposed to—indeed, are required by the Constitution—to speak *for* us. Instead, they're speaking *over* us. I developed the concept of "crashing the club" as a way to give some shape to the blossoming movement toward inclusivity. It's a sentiment that has taken hold of the electorate, and I developed the concept of crashing the club as a way to capture the essence of the movement.

So far, the Tea Party has been at the movement's core. But that's a bit of a chicken-and-egg conundrum: Is the Tea Party truly representative of the movement, or is the Tea Party merely the establishment's way of getting in on what's hot now. In other words, is it possible that the Tea Party is, for all its chatter about revamping politics, just another arm of the establishment?

I say yes. The Tea Party is, I'm afraid, just the Republican Party by a different name. The leaders of the Tea Party are themselves establishment heroes, good ole boys every one of them. What happened is that some key politicians with key connections had a rare bit of forethought, and seeing that Americans are tiring of the establishment, created the Tea Party to capitalize on the cultural zeitgeist. Basically, the Tea Party was formed as a way to leverage the traction of the anti-good ole boy sentiment.

Don't get me wrong…I believe in the tenets of the Tea Party. I believe in the concepts the Tea Party purports to stand for—liberty, justice, and independence. But those aren't partisan ideals, are they? Those are *American* ideals! Every political party—the Democrat Party, the Republican Party, the Libertarian Party…hell, even the Green Party—holds itself out as a bastion of liberty and justice and independence. The reason for that is because the leaders of every party know that those are the ideals that resonate with American voters…and so the party leaders turn into talking points those very ideals.

There's nothing wrong with the Tea Party, at least in theory. But the reality is that the Tea Party is just the Republican Party in disguise. After years of running as Republicans and then leading like liberals, so-called conservatives lost the trust of the American people. The Tea Party is the elites' way of duping voters into thinking that just because the label has changed, so has the product.

Which is all to say that the Tea Party looks like a club-crasher's safe haven, but really it's just another den of iniquity.

In fact, of all the unwelcoming reception I got during my campaign, perhaps most belligerently unwelcoming were Tea Partiers. Buoyed by their own traction, they tried to bully me by declaring themselves the gatekeepers of the political underground. In that way, some in the Tea Party have situated themselves as the be-all-end-all of political reform. The whole thing reminds me of the dorky girl who grew up to be drop-dead gorgeous: Chip-on-the-shoulder, look-at-me-now.

If you don't believe me that the Tea Party is largely a Republican guise, just look at the way the GOP has allied itself with the Tea Party movement. Practically every Republican incumbent who's up for re-election hails himself as "Tea Party before Tea Party was cool." If that were even remotely true, though, Republican officials wouldn't now be finding it necessary to rebrand themselves.

And make no mistake, branding is the very essence of establishment politics…and so it must necessarily be the very essence of anti-establishment politics. Remember that a few pages back I promised to discuss the art of aggravating without alienating? Well, I've finally meandered my way back to that topic.

So listen up.

It's popular to decry the lack of reformers in politics, but the reality is that the political field is full of reform-minded candidates. The problem is that those candidates are rarely elected.

That's not surprising, considering the establishment mite dedicated to defeating reformers.

So there are plenty of good candidates, but *because* they're good candidates they're easily squashed by status quo defenders. Which actually wouldn't be a problem if those reformers knew how to parlay electoral defeat into a platform for change. Unfortunately, reformers tend not to be dimensional in their efforts. Most of them forget that there's more than one way to skin a cat, so to speak.

I developed the concept of club-crashing to remind reformers that losing the battle doesn't have to mean losing the war. That's where the art of aggravating without alienating comes in. To make more than just an ephemeral splash, a club-crasher has to be dynamic.

Squashed by the establishment? Fine—write a book about it.

I'm not necessarily being literal, of course, but you get my point.

Dynamism means figuring out how to make people enjoy disagreeing with you. I'll be up front in admitting that I had a hard time understanding that.

If you spend all your time courting your supporters and arguing with your detractors, all that will happen is nothing. What you have to do—what I learned the hard way—is to court your detractors.

I'm absolutely not suggesting that you suck up to the political elite. I'm not even recommending triangulation at all.

By "court your detractors" I mean that you should disagree with them in a way that engages their egos. A method that is both sincere and effective is to declare to them over and over again that you see them as the establishment. They'll tell you you're wrong, they'll tell you they too seek reform, but secretly they'll enjoy being considered part of the political elite. Because even the goodest good ole boy is constantly worried that he'll fall off the establishment's radar. So by framing your disagreements with them in those terms, you'll flatter them. And then they'll seek you out for further disagreements, because disagreeing with you will make them feel validated and secure.

The efficacy of this method reminds me of a slim woman who, when told by her friends how enviably slim she is, prattles on and on about how she's not really slim at all. She's happy as hell that you think she's skinny, but she'll try her best to tell you how wrong you are.

The same goes for members of the political elite.

I deploy this method all the time on Facebook and in newspaper op-eds. By framing my disagreements with establishment members in a way that makes them have to defend themselves as non-elite, I gain access to the system without kowtowing to it.

Usually this goes a little something like this: I call out a person for some political misstep, throwing in a little something about their affiliation with the political elite, and they fire back a retort about me being politically correct and therefore unable to see the genius of their ways.

See that little trick right there? The reference to political correctness? That's how you know you're on the right track.

When the establishment characterizes me—*me*!—as politically correct, I know I'm beating the good ole boys at their own game. It's kind of like that really brawny quarterback who constantly makes gay jokes, yet is eventually caught in a compromising position with the water boy

...all along, he was trying to deflect attention from his own perceived weakness.

The same goes for members of the political elite. When the establishment—itself a bastion of political correctness—accuses a club-crasher of being PC, what's happening is that the political elite is scrambling to redefine itself. I've seen this exact scenario happen time and time again in the past year or so, which I take as a positive sign: The anti-establishment wave has put the good ole boys on the offensive, which can only mean we're winning.

Take for example Thaddeus McCotter, Congressman from Michigan and current Republican presidential candidate. I have high hopes for Rep. McCotter. Not for president—he's not going to win. I have high hopes for him as a club-crasher. Along with Texas Congressman Ron Paul, McCotter could very well be the second club-crasher in presidential politics. (The fact that there's not one but two anti-establishment presidential candidates speaks to the nation's readiness to break from politics as usual.)

Anyway, McCotter has come under scrutiny from the establishment for, among other things, featuring a black bride and groom on a video that runs on his campaign web site. The Republican political elite decry the video as a politically correct kowtowing. Of course, ordinary people easily read between those lines: It's politically correct to throw around the term "politically correct."

What's interesting about McCotter is that he has avoided defining himself in accordance with the Tea Party movement, even though his hardcore conservative credentials align with Tea Party ideals. This indicates to me that McCotter has his eye on the ball in a way that could make him relevant beyond the 2012 election. It also indicates to me that McCotter has some understanding that a club-crasher has to find a way to transcend fringe appeal, which is where Ron Paul falls short. (Don't get me wrong...I love Ron Paul and his policies, but the fact is that he identifies so well with his supporters that he can't quite translate his appeal in a way that makes him everlastingly relevant.) McCotter, for his part, appeals to the Tea Party crowd without overly telegraphing his libertarian credentials. That's especially important for a candidate who, like McCotter, is sure to lose his election. For a club-crashing candidate, electoral loss is almost guaranteed...and so the goal must be to not only keep but to grow one's audience even after the election fever dies down.

It's for that reason that I avoided aligning with the Tea Party movement during my race. Pigeon-holing myself as a Tea Party fanatic would have probably helped my campaign, but it would have been detrimental to my post-election relevance.

To be sure, political expediency is today a huge handicap. It's in that way that the Tea Party has redefined what it means to be a successful politician. It's no longer the case that politicians who play it safe and toe the line will progress politically.

Consider again Congresswoman and presidential contender Michele Bachmann. Bachmann's entire Congressional 1 career has been defined by a quixotic defiance that, while certainly admirable, led to a political record that's mostly blah. Since being elected in 2006, she has spearheaded no significant legislation. In fact, even her most benign and insignificant proposals have failed to get support from her Congressional colleagues. Yet, despite her stark and unremarkable political track record, she has eclipsed even the inveterate Mitt Romney. That's why her name so often punctuates this book. She is by any traditional measure an ineffective legislator, yet it is because of and not despite her inefficacy that she's poised to be president. She's so far struck that delicate balance between renegade and reformer, and by shifting between those roles she has out-maneuvered the establishment.

There is one area where the elite can't be out-maneuvered, though: Money. The establishment's financial resources defy competition. Simply put, if it's purely a money game, the elite can't be beaten. But it's *not* just a money game—not anymore. You can't win an election without spending money, but you can make a difference on a shoestring budget. In fact, several of the lessons in this book are at their core examples of how to compete with the establishment's vast resources.

It's not easy, though. Though my former opponent and I raised almost the same amount of money, he easily pulled ahead of me when he received $24,000 in an elaborate pay-to-play scheme. That's right...the establishment contributed $24,000 to his campaign in an alleged exchange for his vote on a particular issue. (That particular issue, by the way? A sales tax increase.)

Had my opponent not received that "dirty" donation, would I have won the election? You know, I honestly don't think so. But regardless of outcome, the establishment's money game is a big part of what has soured ordinary Americans to the political process.

The hope is that social media will eliminate the need for gobs of money. Just about every discussion regarding campaign finance reform revolves around whether the Internet is a solution. Social media is free, after all, and it is far-reaching, immediate, and completely customizable in terms of messaging. Still, I'm not entirely sold on it. I certainly believe social media is outrageously valuable to a club-crasher, but my concern is that it can easily become circular and self-limiting. What I mean is that a lot of networking outlets—Facebook in particular—filters content according to what the user views repeatedly. So it's likely that the only people who have easy access to your posts are the ones who already agree with and support you. Remember my warning about ignoring your detractors and courting your supporters? Social media is very susceptible to that.

The risk there is that it's easy to get distracted by the impression that everybody agrees with your message. Since your detractors likely aren't seeing what you're saying, you get feedback only from your fans. And, as I've warned throughout this book, that's no way to build a brand. Relying on the Internet to spread your message is absolutely effective, as long as you don't rely on it to the exclusion of other avenues of exposure.

For a club-crasher, social media is most valuable in terms of the consistency with which you can use it to present your ideas. It's in that way that the Internet can offer an answer to the establishment's money prowess. With its resources, the political elite purchases continuous presence and non-stop promotion of the status quo. It's this relentless presence that is the establishment's most powerful weapon. For the club-crasher, social media can create that same illusion of ubiquity—for free. I think that's the Internet's greatest value to a club-crasher: Free, streaming, continuous exposure. But just remember that the bulk of that exposure will likely be to those who already know and support you…so be careful not to assume that a strong social media presence is on its own enough to combat the political elite.

Ron Paul is a perfect example of both the risk and reward of Internet exposure. During his 2008 presidential bid, all of Paul's traction came from social media. He raised tens of millions of dollars online and rallied all kinds of support. To this day, Paul's Internet presence has eclipsed that of any other politician or candidate. But for all of his online hullabaloo, he got very few actual votes. Nor did he use the power of his Internet brand to build a media empire of books, radio, television, or speaking gigs.

The same thing seems to be happening this time around. For his 2012 presidential bid, Paul has engineered an impressive online following. But the Internet is pretty much where his influence begins and ends. Why? Because a strong social media presence doesn't guarantee audience growth. In fact, because of the intrinsic self-limiting nature of social media that I discussed above, it's very easy for the number of supporters to stagnate.

Maybe it sounds like I'm saying that the ultimate goal of club-crashing is to gather as many supporters as possible. Well, yes and no. I don't think it's necessarily important to have a lot of supporters. In fact, as in the case of Ron Paul, you can have a lot of supporters and still have trouble competing with the political establishment. So no, it's not necessary to have a huge number of supporters. What's essential is that

you have the right number of the right supporters.

Before I define what I mean by the "right supporters," first I'll explain how to spot the wrong
supporters.

The first type of wrong supporter is the political
has-been. This is a person who once wielded
some real power in the political realm, but, because of age or circumstances or whatever else,
is no longer relevant. This is a person who has
connections within the establishment—indeed,
the political elite seems to respect him. That's
why it's so easy to get sucked into this person's
web…from all appearances, he seems to have
some pull with the establishment. So then,
what's his interest in you? Why, if he's so well-
connected, does he spend so much time guiding
you and advising you and inviting you to this
function or that? The answer is that he no longer
has a real role in politics, and so he's using you
as a lifeline. He's using you to remain relevant.
You'll know who this person is because he's the
one constantly trying to talk you out of something you want to do, or trying to talking you into something you don't want to do. In that way,
he does double duty: Ingratiating himself to the
establishment by tamping down threats to the

status quo, and at the same time endearing himself to you by mentoring you.

For me, this person happened to be a family friend. Under that guise, he was my hardiest dissuader when I announced my intentions to run for the state House. He advised me to wait two years and then run for Town Council. In the meantime, he wanted me to volunteer for other candidates' campaigns. He referred to that as "paying my dues." I basically told him to go to hell. Ever since, I've watched as he's "taken under his wing" several up-and-comers, stroking their egos about their future political prospects while relegating them to licking envelopes for other people's causes. So far none of them have lost an election like I did, but neither have they scored a book deal, a speaking gig, or a television show—like I did.

The other type of "wrong supporter" you'll meet is the wannabe club-crasher. This person is well-connected with the people on the fringe. He's brazenly anti-establishment. He is often an effective organizer, rallying support for fringe causes and raising moderate funds for marginal candidates. He's generally intelligent, articulate, and conversant with a variety of esoteric subjects. Though his qualifications are indeed legion, he harbors delusions of grandeur that are outsize to his actual capacity to make a difference. Like the political has-been above, this person clings to you as his own personal cause. It's not really about you, His claim to fame usually revolves around past volunteer work with a high-profile politician. Of course there's no way to verify the veracity of that, and even if there was, it probably happened so many years ago that any connections he may have made have died.

For me, this person was a guy whose heart was in the right place but whose head was all mucked up with fanatical ideas and conspiracy theories. He was devastated when I declined his offer to run my campaign—a service he was happy to do for free, which says it all right there.

Actually, I have to be honest and admit that this person did suck me in for a brief while. I agreed to let him manage my campaign because I was desperate for guidance, he seemed to know the ropes, and he wasn't charging me. So what happened?

Well, his first order of business as my campaign manager was to drive me to the state House for a big policy press conference and have me maneuver myself so that I was standing smack-dab in the middle of the action when the news cameras panned from podium to podium. He explained to me that I'd get some free camera time and face recognition. He thought it was absolutely genius…I know because he told me so on the five-hour roundtrip ride to the state capital. I thought it was ridiculous. But I convinced myself that I was so new to the game that I simply didn't know enough to recognize what a brilliant move it was. That's what I told myself the whole way there. The whole way back, what I told myself was that from then on that I would manage my own campaign, because I knew I'd make mistakes but I also knew I certainly couldn't be any more misguided than this guy.

That was a turning point for me. That's when I realized that experience was all that these seasoned consultants had on me, and that even with all their experience most of them lack basic instinct. It was on that day that I took control of my own campaign and quit waiting for somebody to tell me what to do.

That's probably the absolute hardest thing about crashing any club: Deciding to disregard everything except what your own instincts tell you. When I think back to that day at the state House, inching closer and closer to the news cameras, I cringe. It was so off the mark, so absolutely unconnected to my campaign, so ludicrous a move, that I'm embarrassed to say I agreed to do it.

The third and final type of "wrong supporter" is the person who does it all for the nookie, as goes the expression. This person wants to play prince charming to your damsel in distress. In my experience, this is the most common type of "wrong supporter." This is also the one that's most difficult to spot because, even though his motives are plainly transparent, it's easy to be carried away by all the flattery.

You see, the two other types of wrong supporters make your campaign all about it them—they're doing you a favor by showing you the ropes. That's why when this person—an establishment hero, generally—expresses such interest in helping you, it's hard not to get caught up in the flattery.

The important thing here is to remember to keep your eye on the ball. This person will concoct pretexts to spend time with you...often these pretexts will be functions or meetings or introductions that are legitimately relevant to you, and just as often it will be a waste of your time.

The trick is to figure out how to tell the difference.

I myself am still struggling with that part. In fact, one of the biggest mistakes I made during my race was when I skipped out on an invitation-only lobbyist event to which an establishment suitor had gotten me access. I didn't feel like making the long car trip, because I assumed this was just this guy's excuse to spend time with me. That was indeed his main goal, but it turned out that he'd also arranged meetings for me with huge donors. My absence literally cost me thousands and thousands of dollars. That's why I don't label this type of behavior as sexism: I never mind benefiting from some guy's crush on me.

Anyway, like I said, it's important not just to have a lot of supporters but to have some of those be the right kind of supporters. Now that I've described the wrong types of supporters, how about the right kind?

The right kind of supporter, you'll be shocked to hear, is part of the political elite. A good ole boy, in other words. In theory he shouldn't support you, but for some reason he does. Not because he wants to bed you, and not because he's struggling to regain relevance, but just because he thinks you make sense. Or something like that. And maybe he does want to bed you, and maybe he is worried about fading relevance, but neither of those is the basis for his support.

There's really no telling why this good ole boy supports you the club-crasher. And it's precisely because of his establishment chops that he can afford to support you. If he weren't part of the political elite, he'd just look like a fanatic for supporting you.

This person's approval legitimizes you in the eyes of the establishment, and even more importantly, in the eyes of everybody else. Somewhat counterintuitively, you look like a real live club-crasher in light of this good ole boy's support. Suddenly you are the real deal...all because an establishment hero likes you. In the context of his support, your validity is simply acknowledged and accepted. The most interesting thing is that the charm works on both the establishment and the anti-establishment. Everybody accepts you. Oh, half of them still don't like you, but even they don't deny your influence.

Half the people won't like you no matter what, anyway. Half the people will like you no matter what. So really, influence is the only thing we can control.

That's the point of crashing the club—this book, and the concept as a whole.

The bad news is that you can't make more than half the people like you. The good news is that you can't make more than half the people dislike you. Liked or disliked, the question is: Are you being considered?

I developed the concept of "crashing the club" because through politics I've come to believe that it's none of your business what they think of you, it's only your business that they do think of you. On their minds is always a good place to be.